APES AND MONKEYS

Explore the Fascinating Worlds of . . .

CHIMPANZEES
GORILLAS
MONKEYS
ORANGUTANS

by Deborah Dennard
Illustrations by John F. McGee

NORTHWORD PRESS
Chanhassen, Minnesota

© NorthWord Press, 2003

Photography © 2003: K. & K. Ammann/Bruce Coleman, Inc.: p. 81; Erwin & Peggy Bauer: pp. 66, 118, 135, 145, 183; Alan Briere: pp. 68-69, 78-79, 92, 101, 105; Alan & Sandy Carey: pp. 112, 117; Wendy Dennis/Dembinsky Photo Associates: p. 37; Jenny Desmond: pp. 28-29; Gerry Ellis/Minden Pictures: pp. 31, 89; D. Robert & Lorri Franz: pp. 62, 159; Eric & David Hosking/Dembinsky Photo Associates: pp. 126-127; Adam Jones: pp. 15, 149; Frans Lanting/Minden Pictures: pp. 53, 57, 90-91, 111, 165, 184; Ken Lucas/Visuals Unlimited, Inc.: pp. 52, 72-73; David Madison/Bruce Coleman, Inc.: p. 109; Joe McDonald/Visuals Unlimited, Inc.: p. 61; Claus Meyer/Minden Pictures: p. 114; Kristin Mosher/Danita Delimont, Agent: pp. 10-11, 16-17, 38-39, 40-41, 42-43; Stan Osolinski/Dembinsky Photo Associates: pp. 33, 36, 132-133; Fritz Polking/Dembinsky Photo Associates: p. 121; Kevin Schafer/kevinschafer.com: pp. 75, 107, 146; Anup Shah: pp. 4, 6, 7, 21, 24, 25, 30, 34-35, 44-45, 50, 58, 76-77, 96, 99, 115, 124-125, 136, 137, 138, 142, 144, 153, 155, 156-157, 158, 160, 163, 166, 169, 170-171, 172-173, 174, 176-177, 180; Anup Shah/Dembinsky Photo Associates: cover, pp. 8, 12, 19, 46, 86-87, 98, 150-151; Rob & Ann Simpson/Visuals Unlimited, Inc.: p. 18; Norman Owen Tomalin/Bruce Coleman, Inc.: pp. 54, 110; Art Wolfe: pp. 64-65, 71, 106, 122, 129; Konrad Wothe/Minden Pictures: pp. 67, 74, 82-83, 154, 178-179; Shin Yoshino/Minden Pictures: pp. 102-103.

NorthWord Press
18705 Lake Drive East
Chanhassen, MN 55317
1-800-328-3895
www.northwordpress.com

Illustrations by John F. McGee

Library of Congress Cataloging-in-Publication Data
Dennard, Deborah.
   Apes and monkeys: explore the fascinating worlds of chimpanzees, gorillas, monkeys, orangutans / by Deborah Dennard ; illustrated by John F. McGee.
      p. cm. --(Our wild world series)
   Summary: Presents information on the physical characteristics, habits, and behaviors of different species of chimpanzees, gorillas, monkeys, and orangutans.
   ISBN 1-55971-863-3 (hardcover)
   1. Apes--Juvenile literature. 2. Monkeys--Juvenile literature. [1. Apes. 2. Monkeys. 3. Orangutans.] I. McGee, John F, ill. II. Title. III. Series.

QL737.P96D458 2003
599.8--dc21

2002043147

Printed in Malaysia   10 9 8 7 6 5 4 3 2 1

APES AND MONKEYS

TABLE OF CONTENTS

Explore the Fascinating World of . . .

Chimpanzees

Deborah Dennard
Illustrations by John F. McGee

CHIMPANZEES are more like humans than just about any other animal. Scientists have studied chimpanzees, or chimps, as they are also known, very closely. Chimps and humans have similar social structures and behaviors. It is easy to look at chimpanzees and see something that is familiar.

Chimpanzees and humans are both primates (PRY-mates). One way to tell if an animal is a primate is to look at the hands and feet. A primate has 5 fingers on each hand and 5 toes on each foot. A primate has nails on the fingers and toes instead of claws. A primate also has opposable (uh-POE-zih-bull) thumbs.

This chimpanzee is using its opposable thumb to hold a thin plant stalk.

Baby chimpanzees, such as this one, seem to delight in playing with their elders.

Opposable thumbs and opposable big toes are needed for climbing trees.

Opposable thumbs can reach across the hand to touch all of the other fingers. An opposable thumb allows primates to grasp things. Humans use their thumbs to hold things such as pencils. Chimpanzees use them to hold branches, food, and many other things.

Chimps also have opposable big toes. Their big toes can reach across the foot to touch all the other toes. This makes both their thumbs and big toes excellent tools for holding and climbing.

Africa is home to all chimpanzees in the wild. Chimpanzees can live in many different habitats. A habitat may be a forest, a meadow, a desert, a rain forest, or any place where plants and animals live. Chimpanzees can live at sea level or 9,000 feet (2,730 meters) high in the eastern mountains.

The area in red shows where chimpanzees live in Africa.

Male chimpanzees weigh from about 95 pounds (43 kilograms) to about 110 pounds (50 kilograms). Males are about 3 feet (90 centimeters) tall. Females are smaller. They weigh about 70 pounds (30 kilograms) and average only about 2.5 feet (76 centimeters) tall.

All chimpanzees, both male and female, are strong and muscular. All chimpanzees have coarse (KORSE) black hair over most of their bodies. Some chimps have hairy faces. Some chimps have no hair on their faces. The skin of the face may be pink or dark gray or black.

Like all primates, chimpanzees have large heads in comparison to their bodies. This is because they have large brains and are very smart. Chimpanzees have large ears, heavy rounded eyebrow ridges, and flattened nostrils.

Male chimpanzees are large, powerful animals with heavy, rounded eyebrow ridges.

Chimpanzees love to play. One of their favorite games is piggyback!

Chimpanzees have strong arms that are longer than their legs. Their arms and their legs are good for traveling on the ground or climbing in trees. When chimpanzees walk on the ground, they walk on their flat feet and on the knuckles of their curled hands. This is called knuckle walking. Chimps can walk very quickly in this way. They can also balance on their back legs and walk on just their feet, but this is less common and is much slower.

Chimps are a bit clumsy up in the trees. They do not travel as far or as long in the trees as they do on the ground.

Chimpanzees
FUNFACT:

As chimpanzees grow older their hair may turn gray. They may even become bald.

The scientific name for common chimpanzees is *Pan troglodytes*. Pan is the name of the Greek god of the forest who was part human and part animal. Troglodytes refers to cave men. So the scientific name suggests that chimpanzees are like people in some ways.

Common chimpanzees are great apes. Their closest relatives are gorillas and orangutans. All great apes belong to the same family, called the Pongid (PON-djid) family.

Both monkeys and apes are primates, but one difference is that monkeys have tails and apes do not.

Chimpanzees
FUNFACT:

There is a very rare species (SPEE-sees) of chimpanzee called the bonobo, or the pygmy (PIG-me) chimpanzee. It is smaller and darker than the common chimpanzee and lives only deep in the rain forests of the African Congo. There may be as few as 10,000 bonobos left in the world.

Bonobos are also known as pygmy chimpanzees.
They are smaller and rarer than common chimpanzees.

Chimpanzees live in groups called troops. They spend much time
playing, touching, and grooming each other.

Chimpanzees live in groups, called communities or troops, that can be as large as 100. All of the members of the troop know each other, but sometimes smaller units within the troop team up to eat or travel or explore together. After a while, the smaller units join back up with the rest of the troop. Just like with people, some chimps like each other more and so spend more time sleeping, feeding, playing, and grooming together. It is almost as if chimpanzees have friends just like humans.

In each troop there may be chimps that are not as well liked as others. In fact, there are often animals in a troop that seem to actively dislike others. Sometimes one chimpanzee may even be bullied and chased by others. Usually, a troop is large enough that all of the animals can find other chimps to get along with.

Each chimp troop has male leaders. One of the most important things the leaders do is guide the troop and smaller units to search for food. In rain forests there is more food than in other places. Chimpanzees living in rain forests have smaller territories, or areas in which they find food, because they do not have to go far to gather all the food they need.

Food is harder to find in open woodlands and grasslands. Chimpanzees who live in these habitats have much larger territories, because they must travel farther in search of food. The territory of a troop may be about 20 square miles (52 square kilometers). Inside this territory individual chimps or units may claim a smaller area of their own. These individual territories may be only about 1.5 square miles (4 square kilometers). Chimps don't always stay in their own area. Sometimes they will explore the larger troop's territory, too.

Chimpanzees travel mainly on the ground, but they also climb high in trees to find fruit or to take a long look at their territory.

Chimpanzees are omnivores (OM-ni-vorz), which means that they eat both plants and meat. Chimpanzees have been known to eat more than 300 different kinds of food. They may eat as many as 20 different kinds of food in a day.

Fruit makes up about half of chimpanzees' plant diet. They love figs. When these sweet fruits are in season, chimps may eat very little else. When the season changes, the diet of the chimpanzees changes, too. They eat what is available. In addition to fruit, they eat honey, leaves, bark, and stems to round out their plant diet.

Meat is also an important part of the chimpanzees' diet. Termites are a favorite food and a good source of protein. Chimps also eat eggs, baby birds, and even small mammals such as monkeys. Meat is not eaten every day and is mostly hunted when plant food is harder to find.

Chimpanzees are omnivores and may eat as many as 300 different kinds of food, including plants and some meat.

One sign that chimps are highly intelligent animals is that they make and use tools. A tool is any object used in completing a task. Chimps use rocks as hammers to break open hard nuts. They pound open bee nests with heavy, club-like branches in their search for honey. They use pointed sticks to dig insect larvae (LAR-vee) from as far as two feet underground.

Chimpanzees also make tools to gather water. Thirsty chimpanzees spy water trapped deep in holes and crevices (KREV-iss-ez) of tree trunks. They grab a handful of leaves and chew them into a sponge-like mass. With their long fingers they wad up the chewed leaves and dip them in the hard-to-reach water. The leaves act like a sponge and soak up the water. Then the chimpanzee will squeeze the water from the leaves into its mouth.

Chimpanzees
FUNFACT:

It is believed that few animals other than humans and chimpanzees make tools.

Young chimpanzees learn how to use tools by watching adults and by playing with tools, such as this stick.

To catch termites, chimps select a stick or twig to use as a tool. They take off the leaves and sometimes the bark from the stick. Next they place the stick inside the small opening to the termite mound and wiggle the stick inside the mound a little bit. Then they wait patiently. After a few minutes the stick is slowly removed, inch by inch, from the termite mound. The tiny termites are hungrily licked off of the stick and eaten. Chimps use this same method to find and eat ants and bees.

A chimp uses a stick to fish for termites in a termite mound. Tiny termites clinging to the stick will be licked off and eaten.

Chimpanzees also go after larger prey (PRAY). They form hunting bands to stalk, corner, and catch prey such as colobus (COLL-uh-bus) monkeys, baboons, small antelope, and wild pigs. Chimps have the ability to communicate with each other and to work together to get things done. When they see a prey animal, a troop of male chimpanzees may turn into a fierce hunting band.

Different animals take on different jobs in the hunt. Some are blockers. They prevent the escape of the prey. Some are chasers. They race after the prey to send them into a trap of ambushers (AM-bush-ers). The ambushers are the ones who hide and wait for the prey. Then the ambushers rush in for the final kill.

All of the chimpanzees in the troop, male and female, young and old, watch the hunt. They hoot and scream in excitement. When the hunt is done, all of the members of the troop beg the hunters for the fresh meat.

Chimpanzees
FUNFACT:

As the chimpanzees hunt together they use many loud calls and hand signals that communicate to the other members of the hunting band what to do next.

Chimps love to tickle each other. They laugh, pant, and grin as they play.

Chimps spend a lot of time playing. They seem to enjoy being tickled. Mothers tickle their babies, and young and old chimpanzees tickle each other. They show their pleasure by opening their mouths into a playful grin, laughing a cackling laugh, and panting with delight.

Young chimpanzees learn the skills of being an adult chimpanzee through play. They roll stones or sticks or fruits on the ground and throw them high in the air and try to catch them. They play wild games of chase and tree climbing and tree swinging. This helps them gain the strength and coordination (ko-ord-ih-NAY-shun) they will need as adults. Other games include wrestling and a chimpanzee version of "Follow the Leader." This game often becomes a

These young chimpanzees are old enough to leave their mothers and play wild climbing and wrestling games together.

game of chase the leader! In games, young chimps learn who is strongest and smartest, and who will probably grow up to be leaders in the troop.

Playing can be seen in a chimpanzee troop at almost any time, except when it is raining. Chimps seem to dislike water and rain. They sometimes travel many miles out of their way to avoid crossing a river, even a small, shallow one. During rain they sit huddled together or find shelter in the trees. They do not eat or play or do anything except wait for it to stop raining.

Chimps make faces to communicate what they mean:
Playing (top left), frustration (top right), anger (bottom left), and fear (bottom right).

Chimpanzees communicate very well through calls, hoots, screams, and facial expressions (ex-PRESH-uns). Chimpanzees are very noisy. More than 30 calls and hoots have been identified by scientists. Most of these calls seem to have a specific meaning such as fear or alarm or comfort. By studying chimpanzee faces and behaviors, scientists have a good idea of what chimps are "saying" to each other. A grin of fear is a wide-open mouth with lips pulled tightly back to show teeth and gums. An angry face has lips that are pushed forward in a tight pout. Chimps show frustration by pushing their lips into an open-mouthed pout. Play is shown with a smile that may show teeth, but never teeth and gums. These same facial expressions can be seen on chimpanzees in the wild and on chimpanzees living in zoos.

Chimpanzees
FUNFACT:

When they see humans, chimpanzees usually bark out a short, sharp alarm call, then freeze in their tracks. Then, they may remain perfectly still or may try to disappear quietly into the brush.

Mother chimpanzees spend about 5 years caring for their babies.
This small baby is still very dependent on its mother.

Life in a chimpanzee troop is complex and always changing. Much of chimpanzee life is based on who will be leaders and who will be followers. Often this begins at birth.

Female chimpanzees become mature at about 8 years old. After that they have a baby about every 4 or 5 years. The mother devotes herself to caring for her baby for those 4 or 5 years and teaching it the many things it will need to know to be a strong adult.

A chimp baby starts life helpless and very small, weighing only about 3 pounds (1.5 kilograms). All members of the troop are curious about the new baby and want to have a look. It is the mother who decides whether her baby stays close to her or whether others are allowed a peek, or even to touch or cuddle with the baby.

Young babies cling to their mothers' bellies and nurse, or drink milk from their mothers' bodies. They nurse every hour for just a few minutes. As they grow larger they ride on their mothers' backs. They continue to nurse for nearly 5 years.

Riding on its mother's back is a good way for this young chimp to travel.

Soon, riding on mother's back is not only a good way to travel, it is another happy chimpanzee game. The baby may be brave enough to play with other chimps and go exploring or climbing. When it becomes frightened or unsure, it runs right back to its mother and hops on her back.

By age 3 the baby can eat solid food, climb, leap, and chase other young chimps. It also can travel out of its mother's reach. It may even go to other adult chimps and poke, prod, and pull hair. The adults ignore the play, and they simply walk away when they tire of the playful youngster.

By the time the baby is 4, the mother begins to wean the baby, or stop nursing, and make it more independent. She sometimes refuses the baby milk or a free ride on her back. Baby chimpanzees may become angry at this rejection. They might scream or kick. They might cry or throw rocks and sticks. This is the chimp version of a human baby having a temper tantrum! It may be hard for the mother to watch, but the mother knows she must teach her baby to grow up and away from her.

Chimpanzees
FUNFACT:

It takes about 240 days, or 8 months, for a baby chimpanzee to be born. It takes about 270 days, or 9 months, for a baby human to be born.

Baby chimpanzees have pink, hairless faces that turn darker and hairier as they grow older.

31

By about age 5 the babies are weaned and must feed themselves. Young chimps must keep up with the troop and eventually find a mate of their own. By this time the mother probably has a new baby. Throughout a chimp's life, though, it will spend some time with its mother now and then.

Young male chimpanzees form strong partnerships that are very much like friendships. They sometimes fight with each other, yet they know they must remain close and strong in order to protect the troop from being taken over by other male chimpanzees. Male chimps often stay in the troop into which they were born for their entire lives.

Usually every troop has a head male called the Alpha male. He is the strongest and the most willing to show how strong he is by hooting and screaming loudly. He walks around showing his strength by shaking branches. He looks even more frightening when the hairs on his body stand up on end. When the Alpha male displays like this, the other chimps in the troop show their respect for him. They may do this by backing away with their arms outstretched or by coming closer to groom him.

Chimpanzees
FUNFACT:

Chimps may spend hours cuddled together.
They pick through each others' fur, pat or even kiss each other,
and rest, a tangle of arms and legs and heads.

The male leader of a chimp troop is called the Alpha male.
He may scream and hoot and jump up and down to show his strength.

An older male leader, such as this one, may be challenged by a younger male for control of a chimpanzee troop.

Another male in the troop may challenge the Alpha male. If the challenger wins the fight, he may become the new leader of the troop, the new Alpha male.

Sometimes all of the adult males of a troop patrol the borders of their territory to make sure no other chimpanzee troops enter. If two troops meet at the edge of the territory, the meeting may be very noisy. The chimps may hoot and scream, slap the ground, or throw branches, leaves, and rocks in the air. Usually both troops back away into their own territories. Sometimes they fight, and that can be very bloody.

Chimps are strong and fast. They are not afraid to fight. When fighting, they use their long canine (KAY-nine) teeth and powerful molars and jaws to bite. They go out of their way to find heavy rocks and sticks to throw. When chimps "go to war" like this, they are making sure their territories are safe.

Chimpanzees can be very aggressive toward other animals. They are known to scream and hoot and throw rocks and sticks at possible predators (PRED-uh-torz) such as crocodiles, leopards, and snakes. This may scare the predators away.

Chimpanzees
FUNFACT:

Chimps in captivity or zoos have sometimes mistaken ropes and rubber hoses for snakes and have attacked them.

Two chimpanzees may throw rocks and sticks when they are fighting for control of territory or leadership of a troop.

At adulthood, female chimpanzees leave their birth troops. They wander about the savannah (suh-VAN-uh) or the forest in search of a new troop, a new place to call home. Females in a new troop may think the wandering female is an intruder and try to chase her away. Males in the new troop usually see the new female as a possible mate and welcome her. This can cause confusion.

It may take several months for a female to know whether or not she has been accepted into a new troop. Sometimes she may have to wander from troop to troop to find a new home. Once she is accepted by the new troop, she is a member for life.

This young chimpanzee will not have to worry about fighting to defend his troop until he is much older.

A chimpanzee troop's day begins shortly after dawn. When they wake up, they are hungry. Most of the morning is spent feeding and traveling to feeding spots. When the chimps find trees filled with fruit, they hoot and scream and pound on the tree trunks. They are calling the others to come share in the feast.

By noon the troop is tired and ready for a rest. Some chimps simply lie down on the ground to nap. Others climb into the trees or even build nests for naptime. Afternoon rest time lasts about 3 hours.

Sleeping is not the only activity that takes place during rest time. Chimpanzees need close physical contact. They touch and hold each other. This is called mutual (MEW-chu-ul) grooming. With mutual grooming, the chimps are clean and neat-looking and free of parasites (PAIR-uh-sites) and other unwanted pests. Mutual grooming means much more. Grooming is a way of keeping all of the members in the troop in close and peaceful contact. This is an important part of life for chimps.

Chimpanzees groom each other to stay clean and to keep the peace in the troop. Grooming is a way of saying, "All is well."

This mother of rare twin chimpanzees has twice as much work looking after both of her active babies.

By midafternoon the chimps continue in their search for food to try to fill their bellies before dark. This is the time when chimps may hunt for prey. Chimps might also look for termites or else just sit and eat figs and leaves. There is always some playing, too.

As dusk approaches, chimpanzees climb high into the trees and build a nest for the night. The higher the nest, the safer it is from predators. Nest building is a busy time. If the chimps are moving around in their territory, a new nest must be built every night. If the chimps are staying in the same spot, the same nest may be used again.

A chimp asleep in a nest.

To build a nest, a chimp selects a fork in a tree, a place where several strong branches meet. Branches are carefully bent over or broken and pulled in toward the center of the nest. The chimp may use its feet to hold larger branches in place while weaving smaller branches into the nest to hold it all together. If not enough branches and leaves are available, the chimp may leave the tree and gather leaves and branches elsewhere, bringing them back to the nest to finish it. Some nests are just a clump of messy leaves. Other nests are carefully woven, complex structures.

The best nest builders are adult female chimpanzees. They will let their babies of up to about 4 years old share their nests. Babies begin playing at nest building at about 1 year of age. By the time they must begin building their own nests at age 5, they are already good nest builders. Sometimes large male chimpanzees may watch a female build a nest and then chase her away and claim the nest for the night. The female does not object and simply moves on and builds a new nest.

Chimpanzees are at home in the trees or on the ground.
Chimps may find food or build nests in trees.

Young chimps in the wild grow stronger by climbing and playing together.

One hundred years ago there were probably as many as 5 million chimpanzees living in the woodlands and savannahs of central and west Africa. Now, in the beginning of the twenty-first century, that number may be down to 150,000. The number of chimpanzees becomes fewer every day.

Chimps have not always been treated well by humans. Chimpanzees in circuses or roadside zoos may be treated cruelly, fed poorly, and kept in small steel cages. Chimps kept as pets often are rejected when they are no longer little and cute.

Chimpanzees may remind us of ourselves. Only with the help of humans
can they be saved from extinction.

Some humans hunt chimpanzees for meat or capture them to sell as illegal pets. The chimpanzees' greatest threat comes from the problem of too many people and not enough land for both chimps and people. As the forests, woodlands, and savannahs are turned into farms, pastures, parks, and towns, the chimpanzees lose their homes. Without a place to live, they cannot survive.

Chimpanzees are creatures with intelligence, with family ties, and with the ability to communicate and adapt to the world around them. Like people, they show a range of emotions, including fear, anger, frustration, and affection.

With a lot of care and help from humans in saving the homes of chimpanzees, these amazing animals will survive.

Chimpanzees
FUNFACT:

A chimpanzee's life span is less than 50 years in the wild.
In captivity, some chimps have lived to be over 60.

My APES AND MONKEYS Adventures

The date of my adventure: _____

The people who came with me: _____

_____

Where I went: _____

What apes and monkeys I saw:

_____   _____

_____   _____

_____   _____

_____   _____

___

The date of my adventure: _____

The people who came with me: _____

_____

Where I went: _____

What apes and monkeys I saw:

_____   _____

_____   _____

_____   _____

_____   _____

My APES AND MONKEYS Adventures

The date of my adventure: _____

The people who came with me: _____

_____

Where I went: _____

What apes and monkeys I saw:

_____   _____

_____   _____

_____   _____

_____   _____

The date of my adventure: _____

The people who came with me: _____

_____

Where I went: _____

What apes and monkeys I saw:

_____   _____

_____   _____

_____   _____

Explore the Fascinating World of . . .

Gorillas

Deborah Dennard
Illustrations by John F. McGee

GORILLAS ARE SOME of the most fascinating and misunderstood animals in the world. Gorillas may seem fierce because of their large size, but they are actually very gentle. Gorillas belong to a group of animals called primates (PRY-mates). Humans are primates, too.

All primates have some things in common. Primates have 5 toes on each foot and 5 fingers on each hand. Primates have nails instead of claws on their toes and on their fingers. One of their fingers, the thumb, is special because of the way it moves. This special finger is called an opposable (uh-POE-zih-bull) thumb.

Gorillas are often called gentle giants because of their size, their intelligence, and their largely peaceful nature.

Gorilla mothers are patient with their playful babies and with the curiosity of other youngsters.

Female gorillas and young gorillas, like this one, often climb trees.
Adult males do not because of their size.

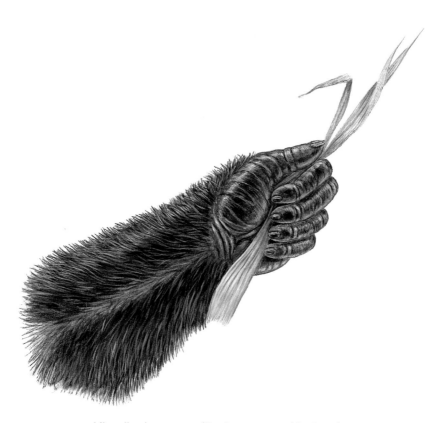

Like all primates, gorillas have opposable thumbs
for holding things large and small.

An opposable thumb can move across the palm to touch all of the other fingers. An opposable thumb lets gorillas and other primates hold small things, such as a blade of grass. Primates can also hold larger things, such as rocks.

Opposable thumbs help gorillas groom each other and climb in trees. Opposable thumbs help baby gorillas cling to their mothers. Gorillas and many primates also have opposable big toes. These come in handy for climbing trees. Humans have opposable thumbs, but humans do not have opposable big toes.

Gorillas are found only in parts of central Africa.

There are over 200 kinds, or species (SPEE-sees), in the order of primates. Gorillas, chimpanzees, and orangutans are so much alike they even belong to the same family, the Pongid (PON-djid) family. That family is also called the Great Ape family, so gorillas are a kind of ape.

All apes come from Africa or Asia.

All gorillas come from Africa. Gorillas are the largest of all of the apes. Apes are primates, and so are monkeys, but there is a difference. Monkeys have tails, and apes do not.

There are two groups of gorillas: lowland gorillas and mountain gorillas. Lowland gorillas live in the dense, lowland rain forests of central and western Africa.

They have short, brownish-black fur. Mountain gorillas are larger than lowland gorillas. They have long, bluish-black fur. They live high in the cloud forests of the Virunga Mountains in the central African countries of Uganda, Democratic Republic of Congo (Zaire), and Rwanda. Cloud forests are rain forests so high up in the mountains that they are often covered with clouds. They are not tropical, because it is not always hot. It can be quite cool, but it does not freeze.

Gorillas
FUNFACT:

Gorillas are the largest and heaviest primates. They can weigh as much as 400 pounds (180 kilograms). Tiny monkeys, called dwarf bushbabies, are the smallest primates. They weigh just 4 ounces (114 grams)!

Lowland gorillas have short, coarse brownish-black hair.

57

Mountain gorillas have thick, long hair that is a dark, blue-black color.

There are many differences between male and female gorillas. Male gorillas are larger and heavier than female gorillas. Males may stand 6 feet (1.8 meters) tall and weigh 350 to 400 pounds (160-180 kilograms). Female gorillas may stand 5 feet (1.5 meters) tall and weigh 200 to 250 pounds (90-115 kilograms).

Adult male gorillas that are 15 years or older have long, silver fur on their backs. They are known as silverbacks (SILL-vur-baks). Female gorillas' fur does not turn silver as they get older. Their fur stays black.

Gorillas
FUNFACT:

Scientists take photos of gorilla faces and memorize the nose prints for identification.

The wrinkles around a gorilla's nose are used like fingerprints to help scientists identify individual gorillas. These wrinkles are called nose prints.

Male gorillas have larger canine (KAY-nine) teeth than female gorillas. In male gorillas, powerful muscles reach from the jaw to a ridge of bone on the top of the skull. This ridge of bone makes a crest. Only males have this crest, so their heads are broader and larger than the heads of females. Female gorillas have smaller, rounder heads.

Gorilla arms are longer than their legs. This is true for all apes. Gorillas have large, round, barrel-shaped chests and potbellies. They are not fat, though. Gorillas are made up of hard, strong muscle. They are very powerful animals.

Scientists who study gorillas are able to tell individuals (in-di-VID-ju-uls) apart by what are called nose prints. The wrinkles, folds, and creases that shape gorillas' noses are just as distinctive (dis-TINK-tiv) as human fingerprints. No two gorillas have the same nose print. No two humans have the same fingerprints.

This lowland gorilla uses his large canine teeth to chew tough, fibrous plants as well as for frightening displays.

Gorillas are social animals. Because they are social, they must be able to communicate. Good communication keeps peace in the family group and keeps the family safe from outside danger.

Gorillas have many ways of communicating. They have many ways to show when they are content or when they are excited, angry, or afraid.

Silverback gorillas may become upset when a strange gorilla comes near their family. When this happens, gorillas scream or growl. They thump their chests and shake tree branches. This makes a loud drumming noise that echoes through the forest. Gorillas always use cupped hands for beating their chests. Cupped hands make a much louder noise than closed fists.

As they pound their chests, gorillas roar and growl and grunt. These noisy displays can be heard a mile away in the forest. Younger male gorillas imitate the actions of their leader, and the noise of the group can be extremely loud.

This lowland gorilla is slapping his chest and hooting to show that he is upset.

The stories of gorillas as fierce monsters came from early explorers who watched these displays of strength in gorillas. However, these frightening shows often take the place of actual fights.

When male gorillas do fight, the combat is fierce. They jab and stab and bite with their huge canine teeth.

Gorillas also communicate quietly. They do not look directly at each other. By glancing away and not staring at each other, gorillas show respect and keep the peace. Another form of peaceful communication is grooming. By grooming each other, or picking through each other's fur, gorillas not only keep their fur clean, but reassure each other that all is well.

Gorillas who live in zoos have learned other forms of communication, such as American Sign Language. This demonstrates the high intelligence of these animals.

Gorillas
FUNFACT:

When beating their chests, gorillas may reach a speed of 10 beats per second.

Gorillas are family animals. Most of the time they live in groups of about 12 to 20. Families can be as large as 36 or as small as 5. One silverback male usually leads a family group, which is called a troop. The family may contain several females and their young.

The silverback male is the protector and leader of the gorilla family. He decides when the troop travels, when it stops to feed or rest, and where it spends the night. He will even die protecting his family, if necessary.

Most of the time, life in a gorilla family is peaceful. Young males and females may sometimes quarrel. The silverback male watches from a distance. He only becomes involved if the fighting becomes too noisy or dangerous.

Gorillas
FUNFACT:

The most famous gorilla who knows American Sign Language is Koko. Koko can sign more than 500 words.

Mountain gorillas live in peaceful family troops.

The silver fur on this eastern lowland gorilla's back is a sign that he is a mature adult male.

Within the gorilla family there is an order of strongest to weakest. This is called a pecking order. The silverback leader comes first. He is on top of the pecking order. Other silverbacks come next, then females with babies, and young males whose backs are still black. After that come females without babies. Finally, the youngsters and baby gorillas are at the bottom of the pecking order.

Lower ranking animals show respect to higher ranking ones, often moving out of their way when one wishes to pass. Higher ranking animals get first choice at foods, but all members of the group are well cared for. The silverback leader fathers most of the babies in his troop.

When two strange gorillas meet in the forest, they may scream, pound their chests, or charge at each other.

A silverback male usually guides his family for many years. Gorillas live to be as old as 40, so the members of a gorilla family may spend many years together. When a silverback leader becomes too old or too weak to lead his group, he may be challenged by a younger, stronger silverback. The challenge from the younger gorilla can become noisy and frightening. The two gorillas charge each other, baring their teeth and growling angrily.

The change from one silverback leader to another looks and sounds more violent than it really is, though. In fact, the old leader often stays on as a group member, following the directions of the new silverback leader.

One silverback male is usually the leader of a family, watching over everything
they do, and deciding when and where the family eats, travels, rests, and sleeps.

Female gorillas become adults when they are about 8 years old. They leave the family they were born into and search for a new family. All of the gorillas in the new family decide whether to accept the new female. The silverbacks get so excited they beat their chests and shake tree branches. Sometimes silverbacks may fight each other over the arrival of the new female. All of the gorillas hoot and scream as the new female approaches because they do not know yet if she will become one of their family. If the gorilla family accepts the newcomer, she will have a home for the rest of her life. If they do not accept her, she will wander through the forest looking for another family.

Sometimes male gorillas live alone, or a group of young males live together for a few years until they are older. Some lone males and females may even start completely new families.

One of the ways gorillas help each other is by baby-sitting. A mother with an infant may allow another female to take care of her baby during long daily rest periods. The baby-sitting gorilla acts like an aunt or older sister. She grooms and gently plays with the baby and keeps the baby out of trouble.

This baby-sitting behavior is very important. It teaches the baby to accept all members of its family and to be a more social animal. It teaches young females how to take care of babies. This allows them to practice for the day when they will have babies of their own. It also allows the baby's mother to get some rest.

Babies are often at the center of the life of a gorilla family. All members of the gorilla family show interest in new babies. Even males want to touch and sniff newborns.

Gorillas adopt orphaned baby gorillas. Sometimes even a huge silverback will care for an orphaned youngster, sharing his nest and his food and providing safety and comfort to the little one.

Like human babies, gorilla babies take a long time to grow up. They spend a lot of time learning to survive as an adult. It takes about 4 years for a baby gorilla to live without the constant care of its mother.

Gorillas
FUNFACT:

Human babies weigh about 7 pounds (3.2 kilograms) when they are born. Gorilla babies weigh only about 4 pounds (1.8 kilograms) at birth but grow to be as much as 2.5 times the size of humans.

Wild celery is a favorite food of mountain gorillas.
This baby is too young to eat solid food yet.

Most female gorillas are excellent mothers and care for their babies for many years.

Life in the forest is difficult and dangerous. As many as 40 percent of all baby gorillas die in the first 4 years of life. They may get sick or fall while climbing a tree, or they may be illegally hunted by humans.

Adult female gorillas usually have only 1 baby every 7 years. This means it is hard for large numbers of gorillas to be born and grow to adulthood. This is one reason why there are few gorillas left in the world.

It takes a baby about 258 days, nearly 9 months, to grow inside its mother. This is about the same amount of time that a human baby grows inside its mother. Most gorilla babies are born at night in nests made of leaves and sticks. Newborn gorillas have pale pink skin that darkens to black within about a week. They weigh only about 4.5 pounds (2 kilograms) at birth.

When this baby gorilla was an infant, it rode underneath its mother. Now it is old enough to ride on its mother's back.

Experienced gorilla mothers quickly hold their babies close for warmth and safety and to give their babies milk. First-time mothers may not do as well. Often they do not know how to feed their babies milk. They may not even know how to hold them. New babies from first-time mothers often do not live more than a few days.

Very small babies may be held to the mother's chest for protection. Usually, a newborn baby gorilla holds onto its mother's underside as she moves about in the forest. Each day the baby gorilla's grip grows stronger. As the youngster grows, it climbs on its mother's back.

Baby gorillas stay close to their mothers
but are curious about everything around them.

As young gorillas grow, they begin to move away from their mothers and explore their forest homes.

Baby gorillas grow physically very quickly but need time to learn all it takes to be a gorilla. When they are about 9 or 10 weeks old, they can sit up alone, and they begin to eat solid food. After 4 months, baby gorillas can walk on all fours like adult gorillas. Soon after they can walk, babies begin to play with the other young gorillas in the family.

Young babies often run back to their mothers for comfort. Older babies wrestle and play with each other. This helps them gain strength and coordination (ko-ord-ih-NAY-shun). By playing, they learn the physical skills it takes to be a full-grown gorilla.

Gorilla youngsters may play noisily in pretend battles. They may quietly explore the world around them by touching, smelling, and tasting everything from sticks to flowers to caterpillars. Like human babies, gorilla babies are curious about everything. They learn by experimentation (ex-per-i-men-TAY-shun) and by imitation (imm-i-TAY-shun).

These gorillas pause to rest before moving on to
feed some more and find a place for the night.

A gorilla troop's morning begins shortly after dawn when the head silverback wakes everyone. The morning is spent in feeding and finding food. If there is not much food, the troop may travel a long way. If there is a lot of food, they may move very little.

Midday means naptime for the adults and play time for the youngsters. Games are often rough and noisy but are still playful. Sometimes youngsters poke, prod, and pull on their elders who are trying to sleep. This does not bother adult gorillas. Usually they just ignore the youngsters and pretend to sleep.

During the rest period gorillas clean and groom their own fur. Mothers make sure their babies are well-groomed. Mothers use their fingers and fingernails to comb through their babies' hair. They lick or gently nibble out any dirt or insects in the hair. They touch and pat and cuddle their babies. Gorillas often make low coughing noises during grooming. It is signal that everything is okay.

Gorillas
FUNFACT:

Gorillas are so large that a footprint left behind may measure as long as 12 inches (30.5 centimeters).

This gorilla is using his opposable thumb to eat some wild celery.

Fields of crops are planted so close to the gorillas' forests that gorillas are sometimes seen in a field such as this one. Farmers may consider gorillas to be threats to their crops.

After the midday rest time, gorillas usually travel and eat until early evening.

A gorilla troop's territory each day is not very large, but over a year gorillas may travel far in search of food. Because of the dense forest in which gorillas live, it is difficult for scientists to know much about gorilla territories. Some studies show gorilla territories are only about 1.5 square miles (about 4 square kilometers). Other studies show their territories to be much larger. There is still a lot to learn about gorillas.

In the evenings, the gorilla troop finds a place to stop for the night. Then they gather plants and sticks that they will use to make nests. This is where the gorillas will sleep.

A gorilla's nest is a circle of plants and sticks pulled toward the center,
making a comfortable circle. Smaller gorillas make nests in trees.
Larger gorillas make nests on the ground.

Gorillas build their nests on the ground or in the lower branches of a tree. The nests are usually not far from the troop's last feeding stop of the day.

A gorilla's nest is a circle of plants and sticks about 6 to 8 feet (1.8 to 2.4 meters) around. Gorillas can build their nests very quickly, in just a matter of minutes.

The lead silverback is the first to begin building his nest. The others in his troop pick spots around him, often according to age and pecking order in the troop.

Babies under 2.5 years old sleep with their mothers. All other gorillas sleep alone.

Gorillas
FUNFACT:

Scientists study the sleeping nests left behind by gorillas. They can guess the number of gorillas in a family and even the ages of each of the family members.

His forest home provides this gorilla with shelter,
safety, and all the food he can find.

Gorillas live on a diet of leaves and fruits. They crush their food with their large, flat molar (MOH-ler) teeth. Gorillas eat many types of plants. They eat ferns, shrubs, grasses, vines, trees, and leafy plants.

Gorillas eat just about every part of these plants. They eat the fruits, stems, flowers, shoots, bulbs, leaves, and bark. Gorillas use their opposable thumbs and flexible fingers to gather food.

Gorillas
FUNFACT:

Gorillas do not usually drink water in the wild. Most of the water they need comes from the plants they eat.

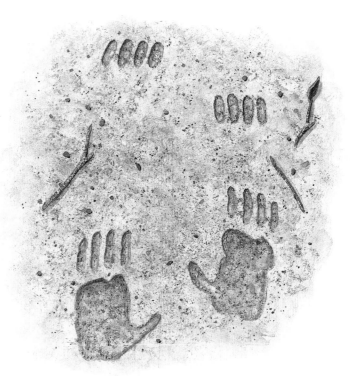

Gorilla tracks show that they walk flat-footed.
They curl their hands into fists to walk on their knuckles.

Gorillas walk using their arms and legs. They curl their hands into fists and lean on their knuckles with each step. This is called knuckle walking. Their feet are placed flat on the ground when they walk.

Gorillas spend most of their time on the ground. When they see tasty fruit and leaves in the trees, gorillas can climb up to get them. They use their hands and feet and climb slowly but confidently up the tree. They can climb as high as 100 feet (30.5 meters) above the ground in search of food.

When climbing down from trees, gorillas move slowly and carefully. They go down with their feet first. Whether they are on the ground or in the trees, gorillas are most comfortable when moving with all 4 limbs. Smaller females and young gorillas regularly explore trees. Adult male gorillas climb in the trees less often and with greater caution because of their heavy weight.

Baby gorillas learn to climb and soon become independent from their mothers.

Gorillas of every age live together in a troop.
Sometimes older sisters help care for younger siblings.

There are very few gorillas left in the world today. Gorillas are an endangered (en-DANE-jurd) species. Mountain gorillas are even more rare than lowland gorillas.

Sometimes humans hunt gorillas for food or for pets. This is illegal. Without protection (pro-TEK-shun) from people, they may become extinct (ex-TINKD). This means they may die out completely.

Gorillas are losing their forest homes. As the human population of Africa grows, more and more land is needed for growing crops, for raising cattle, and for people to live. To make more land for people, land is taken away from gorillas.

Even mountain gorilla babies have thick, long hair.

In 1999 scientists counted about 100,000 lowland gorillas. This is not a large number compared to the number of gorillas there used to be. Most of these gorillas are found in the tiny country of Gabon, in Africa. Gabon has very few people and is mostly filled with forests that are perfect for gorillas. As long as the forests are safe, gorillas are safe.

Scientists counted only about 600 mountain gorillas in 1999. Uganda, Democratic Republic of Congo (Zaire), and Rwanda, where mountain gorillas live, have many, many people. Every year more forest is lost, and more gorillas are lost.

The people in these crowded countries often go to war with each other. When the people fight, gorillas are often killed as well.

Gorillas are some of the most popular animals found in zoos today. While gorillas thrive best in the wild, zoo gorillas are important to the survival of all gorillas. They help teach scientists about gorilla behavior.

Once considered ferocious, gorillas are now often called the gentle giants of the jungle. If their forest homes can be saved, then gorillas can be saved. As long as there is rain forest that is safe from people, there will be gorillas in the world, and the gentle giants will live on.

My APES AND MONKEYS Adventures

The date of my adventure: _____

The people who came with me: _____

_____

Where I went: _____

What apes and monkeys I saw:

_____   _____

_____   _____

_____   _____

_____   _____

The date of my adventure: _____

The people who came with me: _____

_____

Where I went: _____

What apes and monkeys I saw:

_____   _____

_____   _____

_____   _____

_____   _____

My APES AND MONKEYS Adventures

The date of my adventure: _____

The people who came with me: _____

_____

Where I went: _____

What apes and monkeys I saw:

_____   _____

_____   _____

_____   _____

_____   _____

_____

The date of my adventure: _____

The people who came with me: _____

_____

Where I went: _____

What apes and monkeys I saw:

_____   _____

_____   _____

_____   _____

_____   _____

Explore the Fascinating World of . . .

Monkeys

Deborah Dennard
Illustrations by John F. McGee

MONKEYS ARE THE CLOWNS and acrobats of the animal world. They amuse and delight people with their playful behavior and their expressive (ex-PRES-iv) faces. There is a lot more to monkeys than meets the eye, though. They are intelligent creatures, too.

Monkeys are primates (PRY-mates), just like apes and humans. They have 5 fingers on their hands and 5 toes on their feet. They have opposable (uh-POE-zih-bull) thumbs on their hands. They have opposable big toes on their feet.

An opposable thumb can move across the hand to touch all the other fingers. An opposable big toe can touch all the other toes. Humans have opposable thumbs but not opposable big toes. Monkeys can grasp and hold things with their hands and their feet. They can pick up tiny things. They can pick up large things.

Proboscis monkeys are named for their unusually large noses. The word "proboscis" means nose.

Many monkeys are acrobatic climbers. These baby baboons are comfortable climbing right side up and upside down!

Primate heads are special, too. Their heads are large. Primates have big brains compared to the size of their bodies. Big brains are one of the factors that help to make primates smart. Most monkeys are full-grown in about 7 years. Humans are full-grown in about 18 years. The bigger the brain and the longer an animal is still growing and learning, the smarter it will be as an adult.

Tropical rain forests are the most common homes for monkeys. In rain forests they can find fruit and leaves to eat. They climb and jump and rest in the trees. Some monkeys even swing through the trees.

Not all kinds, or species (SPEE-sees), of monkeys live in rain forests, though. There are many different species of monkeys. They look different from each other. They eat different foods. They live in different places.

Monkeys
FUNFACT:

Monkeys and apes look a lot alike, but there is one big difference between them. Monkeys have tails and apes do not.

This pigtailed macaque uses his bright blue eyelids
to show off to other males and to females.

Some monkeys get all the water they need from the plants they eat.
These langurs are drinking deeply at the edge of a stream.

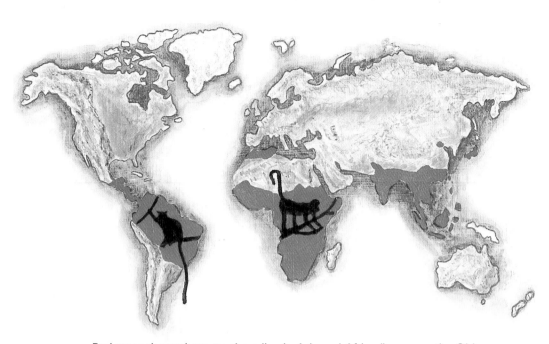

Red areas show where monkeys live in Asia and Africa (known as the Old World), as well as Central and South America (known as the New World).

Monkeys are divided into 2 large groups. One group lives in Central and South America. They are called New World monkeys. There are about 80 species of New World monkeys.

The second big group of monkeys lives in Africa, Asia, and in Europe on the Island of Gibraltar (ji-BRALL-ter). They are called Old World monkeys. There are about 75 species of Old World monkeys.

New World monkeys live only in the tropical forests of Central and South America. The smallest New World monkeys are called marmosets and tamarins. These tiny monkeys are about the size of a small squirrel but have the faces of monkeys. They have fine, silky hair. Some tamarins and marmosets have brightly colored fur. Others have manes like tiny lions, or crests like parrots, or long curving mustaches (mus-TASH-es).

Marmosets are among the smallest monkeys. They live in family groups of 2 to 4 and spend a lot of time grooming.

Tamarins and marmosets are the only monkeys that have claws. They have claws on all of their fingers and toes, except for their big toes. The claws help them to scamper up and down trees by digging into the tree bark. They leap like squirrels from tree to tree.

Tamarins eat fruits, flowers, flower nectar, small snails, lizards, and frogs. Marmosets eat fruit. They also eat tree gum or sap. Their bottom teeth act like special cutting tools to poke holes in tree bark. These holes let the sap, or gum, ooze out of the tree. The hungry marmosets lick up the sap. Tamarins can tell when other tamarins have been at a sap hole and move on to make their own sap holes.

Monkeys
FUNFACT:

Most monkeys have fingernails instead of claws.

Many tamarins and marmosets have showy patches of hair, crests, tails, and colors. These emperor tamarins sport some of the longest mustaches of all primates.

Black-tufted marmosets are always on alert to protect their small families.

Tamarins and marmosets live in many types of forests. They live in wet rain forests. They also live in dry forests where there are no leaves on the trees for about half of the year.

Other tamarins are found in brush lands. Brush lands are places where grasses, bushes, and shrubs grow tall, but where there are very few trees. Sometimes different species of tamarins live together and share the trees and plants. The emperor tamarin, with its large mustache, lives side by side with the colorful saddle-backed tamarin. The saddle-backed tamarin gets its name from the markings on its fur in the shape of a saddle. These two types of tamarins keep in touch in the dense rain forest with their high-pitched squeaking calls. Together they find the ripe fruits and defend their territories from other tamarins.

A capuchin monkey uses its opposable thumbs
as it unrolls a leaf to find a caterpillar to eat.

Capuchin (KAP-yeh-shen) monkeys are another species of New World monkeys. Capuchins are very intelligent and have unusually large brains for primates of their size. They eat fruit, like other New World monkeys. They also eat palm nuts that they crack open by banging on the trunks of trees.

Fruit and palm nuts alone do not provide enough protein, so capuchins also eat insects and snails. They even eat caterpillars. Capuchins find them by carefully unrolling the leaves where caterpillars may be hiding.

Capuchin monkeys are found from Honduras in Central America all the way down to the southern tip of Brazil in South America. Their territory is larger than that of any other New World monkey.

Capuchin monkeys use their tails for many different things like climbing and swinging, and for grabbing and carrying things like fruit and nuts. These strong and flexible tails are called prehensile (pre-HEN-sill) tails. A prehensile tail can be wrapped around a tree branch to help in climbing. A prehensile tail can even support a monkey's whole weight.

White faced capuchin monkeys are very intelligent.
Some have been trained to assist people with disabilities.

These three squirrel monkeys are scampering through well-marked treetop highways in their daily search for food.

Squirrel monkeys are small, graceful New World monkeys that live in groups of as many as 40. They scamper easily in the highest treetops. They often take the same paths through the tops of the trees in their daily search for food.

There are many monkeys larger and stronger than squirrel monkeys, but squirrel monkeys find strength in numbers. Much larger monkeys, like spider monkeys, will not challenge a group of squirrel monkeys for a tree rich with fruit. Squirrel monkeys also snatch up worms and caterpillars from the trees, eating them as they go.

Squirrel monkeys live in a variety of habitats: rain forests, dry forests, and palm forests. They even live near people and raid farms for food. In parts of South America they are called *maicero* (my-SAYR-o), or maize eater, because they steal corn from cornfields.

Spider monkeys are the largest of all of the New World monkeys. They can swing and climb through the trees with their arms and prehensile tails. Spider monkeys have much smaller thumbs than other monkeys. Instead of using thumbs, they use their long, hook-like fingers to hold on to branches. This is very unusual, because most primates have long opposable thumbs.

Monkeys
FUNFACT:

Only New World monkeys have prehensile tails. Old World monkeys do not have prehensile tails.

Some New World monkeys like this spider monkey have prehensile tails that act like an extra hand or foot.

Howler monkeys often make their loud calls
early in the morning or late in the afternoon.

Howler monkeys are some of the largest of the New World monkeys. The males can weigh up to 25 pounds (11 kilograms). There are 6 kinds of howler monkeys. Males of different kinds are different shades of black, brown, and rusty red. Females are smaller and not as colorful. Their fur is gray brown. Howler monkeys eat leaves instead of fruit. Leaves are tough and fibrous (FIE-brus), which means that they are stringy and hard to chew. Animals that eat leaves must have powerful grinding teeth for chewing the leaves.

Leaves have fewer nutrients (NEW-tree-ents) than fruit. Animals that eat leaves must also have special stomachs to get enough nutrients from the leaves. Leaves take a long time to digest. Howler monkeys must rest while their stomachs digest the leaves.

Howler monkeys have prehensile tails and strong arms. They do not swing through the trees, though. Instead, they climb through the treetops carefully, using their arms and legs and tails for balance.

Howler monkeys tend to stay in one part of their territory for a while before moving on to another part of their territory to look for food. While they are feeding in one small area, they are still protecting the rest of their territory with their hooting calls. The calls can carry for many miles. Because of their loud calls and slow movements, they are one of the easiest monkeys to see in the wild.

Monkeys
FUNFACT:

Howler monkeys are named for the roaring, howling noise they make. They have a large voice box, or larynx (LAYR-inks), that helps make their loud, howling call.

The uakari (OO-uh-car-ee) monkey might be the most unusual looking of the New World monkeys. They have bright red faces and heads. They have no hair on their faces. One kind of uakari has bright red hair. Another kind has long, fuzzy white hair.

Uakari monkeys live in the rain forest of the Amazon River basin. They eat leaves and fruit. They also eat the seeds of unripe fruit. This is an important part of their diet. Scientists know little about this species because they are very hard to find in the rain forest.

Monkeys
FUNFACT:

The only monkeys found in North America live in zoos.

The color of the uakari monkey's face varies from pink to bright red, depending on its mood.

Patas monkeys are excellent runners on the plains of Africa. This baby holds on as its mother scampers along the ground.

On the other side of the world, there are monkeys in Africa and Asia. They are known as Old World monkeys. Some Old World monkeys live in trees, and some live on the ground.

Patas (PAH-tass) monkeys live on the ground. They are found in open savannahs (suh-VAN-uhs), also known as grasslands. Savannahs have very few trees and many different kinds of grasses. Patas monkeys sit up on their hind legs, or haunches (HAWNCH-iz), to scan the grasses of the savannah for danger. When trouble is near, they use their long legs to run away from predators (PRED-uh-torz). Predators are other animals, like cheetahs or lions, that might hunt them for food.

The largest group of Old World ground monkeys is the group of baboons. There are so many baboons because they eat a variety of food that can be found almost anywhere. The more kinds of food an animal can eat, the better chance it has for survival. Baboons eat fruit, seeds, plants, and meat. They dig underground for roots and bulbs. They sometimes hunt small animals. The males are fast and powerful runners and have very large, sharp, canine (KAY-nine) teeth. A group of hunting males can chase down a small antelope. Once they make their kill, they do not want to share, so they fight each other for the prize.

Another reason there are so many baboons is that they can live in many different places. Hamadryas (ha-ma-DRY-es) baboons live in near-desert areas of Ethiopia and Arabia. Gelada (je-LA-de) baboons live in the mountains of Ethiopia. In Tanzania, olive baboons live in the rain forest and on the open savannahs. In South Africa, chacma (CHOCK-ma) baboons live near water and even eat water lilies.

Baboons have arms that are about the same length as their legs. They walk on all fours through the grasslands. When they place weight on their hands, just their fingers touch the ground. They hold their palms up and away from the ground. Baboons have very flat feet that are not very useful for climbing trees.

Olive baboons often cuddle and groom each other in groups.
Grooming helps keep the animals clean and helps keep peace in the troop.

Another type of Old World monkey that lives on the ground is the mandrill. Mandrills are large and are often mistaken for baboons. They live on the ground like baboons. Unlike baboons, they live in thick forests in western Africa. Mandrills live in groups of as many as 700.

Monkeys
FUNFACT:

Mandrills are the largest monkeys in the world. Males can weigh up to 120 pounds (54 kilograms).

Male mandrills have brightly colored faces, which they use to show off to other males or to females.

The largest monkey: mandrill.
The smallest monkey: marmoset.

There are 19 species of macaques (ma-KACKS) living in many different places and habitats in the Old World. Some of them even live near people, so they are easy to spot.

Japanese snow macaques live near people. Food is placed by game wardens in parks and at the edges of the forests where the macaques live. This feeding allows the macaque groups to grow very large. Some macaque groups are as large as 1,000 monkeys!

Feeding by humans changes the natural way that the macaques get their food. This can cause problems in the troop because the macaques learn to fight for food rather than search for food. The strongest female and her family usually get first chance at the food provided by humans.

Monkeys
FUNFACT:

Japanese snow macaques live where winters are long and cold and snow is deep. In the winter, they find hot springs and take long, hot baths.

Japanese snow macaques have such thick, warm fur that they can stand cold winter temperatures and even deep snowfalls.

Some langurs are called temple monkeys because they live near people,
even entering their temples or churches.

The Old World monkeys called colobines (COLL-uh-bines) are quite different from other Old World monkeys. Colobines lives in trees and eat leaves. Colobine monkeys have extra sharp molar teeth to shred the tough leaves into tiny pieces before swallowing.

Colobine monkeys in the Old World live much as howler monkeys in the New World do, eating leaves and slowly digesting them. Howler monkeys have special stomachs for digesting leaves, but colobines are even more unusual. They have 2 stomachs for doing the job.

The colobine monkeys of Asia are called leaf monkeys or langurs (long-GOORS). The Hindu people of India believe that hanuman langurs, also known as temple monkeys, are sacred (SAY-kred). This means they are special and may not be harmed, even if they steal crops from fields. Many of these monkeys live near people, often right in the towns. They are named after Hanuman, a monkey god in Hindu mythology. On certain days of the year these langurs are given food to eat in the Hindu temples. If one is accidentally killed, it is given a funeral and is mourned by the people.

Monkeys
FUNFACT:

Leaves do not have all of the minerals that colobine monkeys need, so to get more minerals, they eat dirt.

All monkeys, both Old World and New World, are social animals. This means they live in groups, or "troops," and like to interact (in-ter-AKT) with each other. Troop sizes can be as big as 1,000, like the Japanese macaques. With other species, troops can be as small as 4: a mother, a father, and their babies. This is very close in size to a human family. No matter the size, living in a troop keeps monkeys safe from predators.

Monkeys live in a variety of family structures (STRUCK-churs). Patas monkeys live in small groups of about 20, with several females and only 1 male. The male does not lead the group, even though he is twice the size of the females. The females lead the group, and the male follows along as a sort of bodyguard.

Red colobus monkeys are leaf-eating monkeys that have 2 stomachs for digesting their tough, leafy food.

Olive baboons travel in large troops across the African plains.
They also enter forests and rain forests.

Some monkey troops are led by a group of females who stay together for their whole lives. Often female leaders have female babies that grow up to be the leaders of the next generation (jen-er-AY-shun).

Other types of monkeys are led by males. Olive baboon males are the strong leaders of their troops. Groups of male olive baboons form gangs that keep all of the other members in line. Within the troop there may be several gangs of males. The males in the strongest gangs are the ones who father the babies of the troop. They decide when the troop will move to find food and water and safety, and when it will stop to rest.

For other baboons, only the largest and strongest male becomes the leader. He is the only one to mate with the females. The leader gets first choice of food and is obeyed by all other members of the troop. Someday a younger male will challenge him. The leader of the troop will be the baboon that wins a bloody battle.

There are different ways in which monkeys and other primates communicate. Most monkeys communicate through sounds and actions.

Monkeys can be very noisy! Monkeys cannot use words like humans. Monkeys communicate by making different sounds. Squirrel monkeys keep in contact by making peeping noises when they cannot see each other in the dense rain forest. The farther apart they are, the more they peep. They twitter as a signal to move on. They make a low chucking noise when they are together to signal that all is well.

Marmosets communicate with trilling noises that sound like bird calls. Howler monkeys use pulsing, roaring calls that travel through the forest. Their throats balloon out as they howl, making the roar even louder and making the sound travel farther.

Vervet monkeys, an Old World species, have special alarm calls that tell other members of the troop when there is danger nearby.

The danger can be an eagle flying overhead, or a python slithering along the ground, or even a leopard in a tree. Scientists have studied vervet monkeys and have recorded their calls.

A large male baboon may smack his lips loudly or scream to show his strength. The scream, along with an open mouth to show huge canine teeth, is often enough to keep away intruders or to make a younger baboon behave.

Colobus (COLL-uh-bus) monkeys use a bellowing sound to keep their distance from other colobus monkeys. This helps them avoid getting too close to each other and fighting over food sources. They call to show where they are. As long as they hear each other but do not see each other, they are safe. Once two troops of colobus see each other, they stop roaring and make noise by shaking branches until one troop leaves.

Squirrel monkeys are so small and light that they can even climb out onto delicate palm fronds.

Monkeys communicate by sound. They also communicate with their faces. Monkeys have many facial expressions (ex-PRESH-uns) with meanings that other monkeys understand.

Monkeys often show an alert face with open eyes and lips that are slightly open. When they are ready to attack, monkeys open their eyes wide, and their mouths become a tiny slit.

When they are frightened, many monkeys open their eyes wide and open their mouths so wide that all of their teeth and their gums show. Monkeys show weakness by looking down with their eyes barely open. Their mouths are open enough to show their teeth. To a human, it looks like a small smile. A baby may beg with its mouth pushed forward in the shape of an "O."

Monkeys
FUNFACT:

**Two monkeys greeting each other may show
their pleasure by sticking out their tongues,
opening their eyes wide, and making a sucking
or kissing movement with their mouths.**

Monkeys communicate many things with their faces:
a greeting (top left), begging (top right), fear (bottom left), and alertness (bottom right).

All members of a baboon troop want to smell, touch, and groom the new baby.

Touching is an important way to communicate. Monkeys spend a lot of time touching, or grooming, each other. Monkeys use their hands and sometimes their teeth to pick and comb through each other's hair. As they groom each other they remove dirt and insects, such as fleas. Grooming helps to keep the troop clean and healthy. Touch also can be very comforting, so grooming sends the message that all is well in the troop.

Monkeys groom each other in different ways. New World titi (ti-TEE) monkeys sit in pairs with their tails curled like a rope as they groom. Others, like some macaques, groom each other only at arm's length.

Grooming may show a monkey's "pecking order," or importance, in a troop. In some troops, the females groom the male leader for a long time. The male grooms back, but only for a short time. In this example, the male is higher up in the pecking order than the females.

Younger male monkeys may groom older, stronger males to show their respect for their leaders. Females may groom each other to show their friendliness. Males may groom females they hope will become their mates. And often all members of a troop groom babies and youngsters to show their interest and concern. Grooming helps the young monkeys learn the ways of the troop.

Monkeys
FUNFACT:

"Monkey see, monkey do" is an
old expression, but it is true.
Monkeys learn by looking and copying.

These Japanese snow macaques are warming themselves
in natural hot spring waters in the middle of winter.

Monkeys learn by copying the things they see other monkeys do.
This baby baboon is taking its first few steps away from its mother.

Babies are some of the most important members of a monkey troop. Baby monkeys and other young primates spend a long time in childhood. Babies depend on their parents and the other adults of the troop for almost everything. During these childhood years monkeys learn the many things they need to know to be an adult monkey.

Monkey babies are helpless when they are born. They depend on their mothers for everything, from getting milk to getting around. A tiny baby usually travels by holding onto its mother's belly or chest, often helped by the mother's comforting hand. A larger baby usually travels on its mother's back.

Marmosets are monkeys that do not depend on their mothers for very much. These tiny monkeys go to their mothers only for milk. The rest of the time their father carries them, grooms them, and cares for them.

In no time at all, the baby baboon has grown enough to play with other babies, away from the constant touch of its mother.

Squirrel monkey babies spend up to 2 weeks taking care of themselves. Their mothers do not seem to notice their babies at all for the first 10 days. The babies must hold on to their mothers by themselves with their tiny, strong hands and feet. They must find their mother's milk on their own. When the babies are close to 2 weeks old the mothers begin to pay attention to them and care for them.

Most primates take care of their babies as soon as they are born. No one is sure why squirrel monkeys do not.

Young monkeys, like young people, go through many stages of growth. They start by needing their parents for everything. As they grow, they become more and more independent. They are learning all the time, and then one day they will be able to survive on their own.

Monkeys like these langurs are dependent on the places where they live for their safety.
Only there can they find the food and homes they need to survive.

The world of monkeys is a world of variety. No two species of monkeys are quite the same. No two monkeys are quite the same. Like people, they have their own personalities. Monkeys are intelligent animals that live in many places and in many ways. Their appearance can range from cute to frightening. Their behavior can be gentle or aggressive, playful or serious. What is true about all monkeys is they always surprise and amaze.

Monkeys need the protection (pro-TEK-shun) of people. Many monkeys are endangered (en-DANE-jurd) or threatened (THRET-end). Animals that are threatened may be in trouble if something is not done to help them right away. Animals that are endangered are already in trouble. Without protection, they could become extinct (ex-TINKD), or completely disappear.

The main reason that monkeys are in trouble is the loss of their territory. As people use the land where monkeys live, monkeys lose their homes. Without homes, they cannot live.

Can monkeys find safety in the world they share with people? Yes, with the help of caring people, monkeys and the places where they live can be saved.

One of the most important things to help save monkeys is to learn about them. Scientists are continuing their research so that people can better understand and learn from these fascinating animals. It is not just up to scientists, though. Anyone who loves nature and wildlife can learn about the primates with which we share our world.

Scientists are learning more about primates every day. There were 38 new species of monkeys found by scientists between 1990 and 2001. Most of those were found in the Amazon rain forest of Brazil. Two tiny species, found in 2001, are called the Bernhard's monkey and the Stephen's monkey.

No one knows for sure how many unknown species of monkeys are hiding in the rain forest. Unless those forests are saved, some species of monkeys could become extinct before anyone even knows they were there.

My APES AND MONKEYS Adventures

The date of my adventure: _____

The people who came with me: _____

_____

Where I went: _____

What apes and monkeys I saw:

_____   _____

_____   _____

_____   _____

_____   _____

The date of my adventure: _____

The people who came with me: _____

_____

Where I went: _____

What apes and monkeys I saw:

_____   _____

_____   _____

_____   _____

_____   _____

My APES AND MONKEYS Adventures

The date of my adventure: _____

The people who came with me: _____

_____

Where I went: _____

What apes and monkeys I saw:

_____   _____

_____   _____

_____   _____

_____   _____

The date of my adventure: _____

The people who came with me: _____

_____

Where I went: _____

What apes and monkeys I saw:

_____   _____

_____   _____

_____   _____

_____   _____

Explore the Fascinating World of . . .

Orangutans

Deborah Dennard
Illustrations by John F. McGee

ORANGUTANS are mysterious creatures. The people of Malay (ma-LAY), which is now known as Malaysia, called the creature *orang hutan* (oh-RANG WHO-tan). This means "old man of the forest." There is a legend about how the orangutan got its name. The story is about a man who owed his neighbors some money. When he could not pay the money back, he hid in the forest. He stayed there so long he became more like the animals of the forest and less like a human. As the legend goes, after a long time his children came to be orangutans. Other Malayan people believed that orangutans were simply another tribe of unusual people.

Some native people in Malaysia believed that orangutans were simply odd-looking people who lived in trees.

This mother Bornean orangutan will spend 7 years taking care of her baby.

145

Male orangutans, such as this Borean male, have fleshy cheek pads that frame their faces and make their heads look large and round.

Orangutans are very unusual. They are the largest arboreal (ar-BOR-ee-al) animals in the world. Arboreal animals live mostly in trees.

Male orangutans weigh 200 to 300 pounds (90-136 kilograms) and are twice as big as females. They are about 5 feet (1.5 meters) tall and have very long arms, short legs, and long hands. Their arm span, the distance from one hand to another with their arms outstretched, may be as wide as 8 feet (2.5 meters). They have bright, red-orange shaggy fur.

Males have fleshy half circles on their cheeks that are called cheek disks or pads. These pads frame the face and make orangutans' heads seem to be very large. The pads are a sign of adulthood. The larger the cheek pad, the more important the orangutan is. To some people, this makes orangutans look very strange.

Orangutans
FUNFACT:

The natives of Borneo (BORE-nee-oh) told stories of orangutans that were so strong they could stand on top of a crocodile and hold its jaws open!

**Orangutans live only on the Southeast Asian islands of Sumatra (left)
and Borneo (right), shown in the red areas above.**

Orangutans may live to be about 40 years old in the wild. Orangutans once lived throughout Southeast Asia. Now they only live on the Southeast Asian islands of Borneo and Sumatra (Sue-MA-tra). Orangutans from Borneo and Sumatra are separated by the open waters between their islands. Though there are differences between these orangutans, they are still very much alike. They could breed and have babies together. Because of this, scientists call them subspecies. That means they are almost, but not quite, exactly alike.

The scientific name for orangutans is *Pongo pygmaeus*.

Bornean orangutans, like the male shown here,
have thinner hair than Sumatran orangutans.

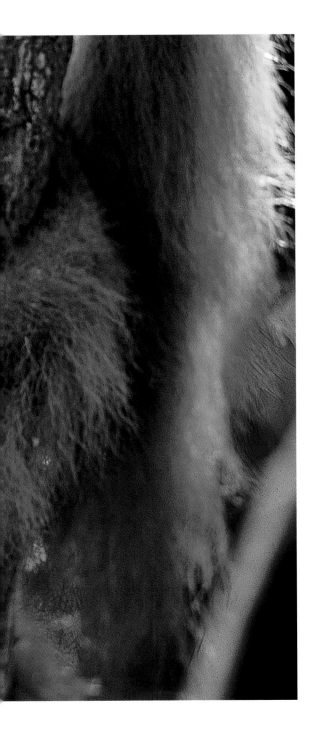

Orangutans on Sumatra have thicker fur than the orangutans on Borneo. Scientists think the reason may be that it is colder on Sumatra, and orangutans there need more fur to keep them warm. Sumatran orangutans have thin, diamond-shaped faces, orange mustaches (mus-TASH-es), and a small throat sac. Bornean orangutans have larger, rounder cheek pads, a square shaped face, and a very large throat sac. The throat sac allows an orangutan's neck to expand. This lets more air through and makes their calls louder.

The closest relatives of orangutans are gorillas and chimpanzees, but they do not look much alike. However, all three are so closely related they belong to the same family, the family of great apes.

Orangutans' feet are as useful as their hands for gripping things.

All great apes are primates (PRY-mates). It is easy to tell if an animal is a primate. First of all, primates are mammals. Mammals are animals that have hair and are able to nurse their babies, or feed them milk from their bodies. A primate also has opposable (uh-POE-zih-bull) thumbs. An opposable thumb can reach across the palm of the hand for picking up things.

Orangutans have long hands and fingers and short thumbs that work like hooks. Orangutans also have opposable big toes. This allows them to climb, travel, and hang in trees.

Primates have eyes that face forward on their faces. They have large heads and brains. Primates are very intelligent creatures. Orangutans, like monkeys, gorillas, chimpanzees, and humans, are primates.

Like all primates, orangutans have opposable thumbs.

Orangutans live in different habitats. A habitat is a type of environment where an animal lives. An orangutan's habitat can be a tropical rain forest, a swamp forest, or a high tropical mountain forest. There are perhaps only 25,000 orangutans left in the wild. The rest live in zoos.

Orangutans
FUNFACT:

Orangutans are the only great apes that live in Asia and the only great ape to spend most of their time in trees.

Orangutans live in wet, green places like rain forests and swamp forests. They get most of the water they need from the food they eat, but like this young one, they may come down to a stream for a drink.

This orangutan is chewing on a long, green plant stalk, but fruit is the biggest part of the orangutan diet.

Orangutans love to eat fruit. In fact, they are the largest animals in the world to depend on fruit as the most important part of their diet. Scientists have identified about 400 different types of food in an orangutan's diet. More than half of their diet is fruit. A favorite wild food of orangutans comes from the durian (DUR-ee-en) tree. The fruit tastes like sugar and garlic, and is creamy like a pudding. Orangutans also eat leaves, flowers, bark, nuts, and sometimes even eggs. They also eat small animals and insects, such as lizards and caterpillars. Because they eat both meat and plants, they are omnivores (OM-ni-vorz). Meat makes up a very small part of an orangutan's diet, though. It is not nearly as important to them as fruit.

How do orangutans find enough food in the forest to survive? They find food in different parts of the same tall trees. Because female orangutans are half the size of male orangutans, they can climb higher in the trees. That is where they find their food. Male orangutans are so large they cannot climb very high in the trees. They stay lower down in the trees, and that is where they find their food. Rain forest trees can grow to be 100 feet tall (about 30 meters). Males and females can share these same tall trees but never notice each other, except when it is time to breed. Eating in different parts of trees is a way to make sure that all the orangutans get enough to eat.

Orangutans
FUNFACT:

Orangutans do not need to go to the ground to find water. They drink rain that has collected in hollows and holes in the tree branches.

This mother orangutan and her baby are smaller than male orangutans,
so they can climb higher in trees to look for food.

Orangutans travel across the same routes in the forest. They have a very good memory for the location of fruit trees and visit them over and over again. Males may travel as many as 3 miles (4.8 kilometers) in a single day to find food. Females are smaller than males, and they need less food. They stay closer to home and only travel about 1 mile (1.6 kilometers) in a day.

Scientists believe that orangutans are able to remember many details about their forest homes. They can remember where good feeding trees are and the seasons when fruits will be ripe. Orangutans do not just wander through the jungle trying to find fruit trees. They seem to head to certain areas and trees at just the right time. This helps to show how intelligent orangutans are. They have map-like memories of the forests.

Orangutans use their strong, long arms and legs to travel across the routes they know well in the forest. They seem to remember certain trees and when their fruit will be ripe.

Finding enough food is important. Orangutans must eat a great deal of food to feed their large bodies. They may spend half of each day eating, and the other half resting. Sometimes several orangutans gather together, especially if there is a tree with a lot of fruit on it. As many as 8 orangutans have been seen feeding together, but this is very rare.

Orangutans do not appear to be in a hurry. They eat slowly and usually alone. They climb slowly through the tall trees of the forest. Scientists used to think that their slow pace meant they were not intelligent. This is not true. Instead, it helps orangutans to survive. For example, their slow movement is one way orangutans avoid predators (PRED-uh-torz). Because they sit still for long periods and move slowly, orangutans can blend safely into the forest.

This young Sumatran orangutan is old enough to explore on his own but has not yet become an adult.

Scientists used to think that orangutans stayed away from water, but some orangutans, including this young one, seek out water and even play in it.

Orangutans in captivity have helped scientists learn how intelligent these animals are. Like gorillas and chimpanzees, they can learn sign language. They have been known to pick the locks of their cages and always seem interested in what their keepers are doing. They explore the world around them by touching, tasting, and smelling things. Orangutans in the wild have even been known to steal people's backpacks just to have a look inside!

Scientists used to think that orangutans were afraid of water, but this is not completely true. Some orangutans plunge right into jungle streams. Others go out of their way to cross at the shallowest part of the streams. Different orangutans act in different ways around water. Some young orangutans even seem to play in the water.

Orangutans
FUNFACT:

Some orangutans in captivity have learned as many as 150 words in sign language.

Orangutans need good balance to climb high in the rain forest trees. This is no problem, even for 200-pound (90-kilogram) males. Their strong legs and arms are perfect for climbing and balancing.

Orangutans are so strong they can support their entire body weight with any one hand or foot. Their hands are rough and calloused from climbing in the trees, and they can use their feet the same way they use their hands.

Their shoulder joints and hip joints are very strong and flexible. This allows orangutans to stretch and reach for branches. They seem to have no fear of heights and no problem hanging upside down.

Orangutans
FUNFACT:

Orangutans can even eat
while hanging upside down.

Orangutans are strong and climb equally well with their hands and feet.

A mother orangutan uses her body like a bridge so that her baby can cross safely between two trees.

Orangutans move through the trees using their long arms, their long hook-like hands, and their grasping feet. They do not swing quickly between the trees like some other primates do. Instead, they use their arms and legs to bend one tree branch to meet another. This forms a bridge that they can use to climb through the trees. Sometimes an orangutan will even rock back and forth in a tree, causing the tree to bend far enough to reach the next tree.

A mother orangutan with young may use her body to make a bridge. She holds onto one tree with her hands and another tree with her feet. As she closes the gap between the trees, her youngster simply scampers across her back.

It might seem that orangutans find safety in the treetops. This is not always true. In Sumatra, clouded leopards share the treetops with orangutans. These strong predators usually leave large male orangutans alone. However, leopards hunting in the trees sometimes catch sleeping female orangutans. Sometimes large snakes may kill baby orangutans, but predators do not present too much of a danger to most orangutans.

Orangutans in Borneo are more likely to come down to the ground than orangutans in Sumatra. The reason is that there are no tigers in Borneo, so there is safety on the ground. They also may come down to the ground more often because the forest in Borneo is not as thick as the forest in Sumatra. They have to come down to the ground to get from one place to another.

Most orangutans spend most of their lives high in the treetops. This baby seems to be playing as it climbs in a tree.

Very long arms and legs help orangutans to stretch from one tree branch to another and to reach a long way to grab fruit.

Sumatran orangutans spend as much as 95 percent of their lives in the trees because of the thick forests there and because of the danger of tigers. It may sometimes take longer to move around in the trees than on the ground, but for orangutans in Sumatra, it is usually safer in the trees.

Orangutans on the ground do not move around very well, and they walk with their feet curled into fists. The heels of their feet are not well suited for walking flat-footed. They are slower and clumsier on the ground than in the trees. However, some orangutans seem to like it better on the ground. One male orangutan was known to spend as many as 6 hours a day on the ground. Some large males even make nests on the ground. Still, most orangutans spend most of their time in the trees.

One advantage of life in the trees for orangutans is the camouflage (KAM-uh-flaj) of their bright orange fur. It may seem that their fur would be easy to spot in the trees, but it is not. With the bright sunlight and the dark shade caused by the huge trees, orangutan fur blends right into the treetops. Their fur looks a lot like the trees and the plants that grow on the trees.

Orangutans
FUNFACT:

Baby orangutans have light orange fur and pink or white patches of skin around their eyes.

Most primates are social animals and live in groups. Orangutans are different. They spend most of their lives alone. The only exception is a mother orangutan. She may spend 7 or more years caring for a single youngster. Of all primates, only humans spend more time caring for their young.

Although orangutans live alone, their territories overlap. Within the territory of each male there are usually about 4 females. Each female lives alone or with her baby, but away from the male. Females may call softly to their babies, but these calls are not nearly as loud as the calls of males.

Males announce their territory daily with loud, echoing calls. These "long calls" sound something like the roar of a lion and are made louder by the male orangutan's throat sac. This sac inflates to make a stronger sound. The long call can be heard more than a mile away.

Smaller male orangutans know to stay away from these calls because they announce the territory of a stronger, larger male. Females with babies also stay away, but females without babies are attracted by these calls. The long calls may be a way orangutans find each other in the dense forest at mating time.

Except when mother orangutans are caring for their babies,
most orangutans spend much of their lives alone.

Males sometimes fight. They show sharp teeth, bite, and wrestle each other, especially when a female is near.

Sometimes when a female without a baby is near two males, the males fight over the female. They bite and wrestle. Orangutans are so strong that gashes and broken bones from biting and wrestling are common. Orangutans also break off tree branches and throw them to the ground when they fight. They show their irritation by making loud, sharp, sucking noises called "kiss squeaks."

Males show off for females at mating time. Hanging upside down in a tree and making long calls is a favorite thing for males to do to get females' attention. Females like this. The males that please females are the ones most likely to father new babies.

Male orangutans in Borneo stay with their females for only a few days when mating. In Sumatra the males stay with their females for several months until the baby is born. They make sure the mother gets enough food.

A pregnant female is about 50 pounds (23 kilograms) heavier than a female that is not pregnant. This makes it hard to move in the trees and find food. Without a male to scare away other animals, a Sumatran female may have a hard time getting enough food. After the baby is born, the female is lighter. She can move around more easily in the trees to find fruit so the male goes his own way.

An orangutan baby takes about 8.5 months to grow inside its mother. A baby usually weighs only about 4.5 pounds (2 kilograms) at birth. An orangutan mother is very protective of her baby. She seems to stay away from other animals when the baby is very small. Most primates spend a lot of time caring for their babies, grooming them, and feeding them. So do orangutans. Unlike other primates, orangutans almost never play with their babies. They seem to stick to the business of raising the baby.

Baby orangutans weigh about 4.5 pounds (2 kilograms) at birth and are carefully tended by their mothers.

Baby orangutans have pink faces and pink or white circles around their eyes.
They know to stay very close to their mothers.

Occasionally, another lone female joins up with a mother and baby orangutan. This may help a younger female learn how to care for a baby. Females with babies sometimes gather to feed in a rich fruit tree. When these meetings happen, the babies play with each other before following their mothers back to the solitude of the forest. Baby orangutans in zoos may spend much time playing with other babies, but this rarely happens in the wild. Orangutans in the wild, both babies and adults, do not spend much time in play.

For the first year of life the baby must depend on its mother for everything. It clings to its mother's long shaggy fur with its strong toes and fingers. The baby drinks milk from its mother. At about a year of age it begins to eat solid food its mother has chewed and given to the baby.

During this time the baby begins to climb and swing and explore its treetop home, but it is always close to its mother. At about age 7, young orangutans wander off on their own. They may spend some time with other newly independent young adults before they find their own territories and become solitary adults. A young orangutan is not a full-grown adult until its early teen years.

Orangutans FUNFACT:

A female orangutan will have only 3 or 4 babies in her entire 40-year lifetime.

Mother orangutans spend time taking care of their babies
and on rare occasions play with them.

Baby orangutans have been popular pets in some parts of Southeast Asia. The mother is killed to catch the baby. When they are small, baby orangutans are adorable little clowns. Very soon they grow up and become too large and strong to be kept as pets. This can be a problem. What do people do when their pet orangutan is too big to be a pet any longer? Some people just abandon them. Others try to retrain them to live in the forest again. This is not an easy job and does not always work.

Orangutans
FUNFACT:

Most primates groom not only their babies, but also each other. Orangutans only groom their young.

These two baby Bornean orangutans have been orphaned and are being raised by people who will try to teach them to live on their own in the wild.

Orangutans build 2 nests each day. One is for napping during the day and one is for sleeping at night.

Nest building is an important behavior for orangutans. Orangutans build 2 nests every day: a day nest for their naps and a night nest. They build their nests in the fork of a tree. They pile thick branches into a sort of a platform, and then they line the center with leaves. A nest may be as large as 5 feet (1.5 meters) around.

Orangutans often pick nest sites that face west to soak up the last warm rays of the setting sun. Sometimes they

Mother orangutans share their nests with their babies until the babies are about 3 years old.

may choose trees that hang over water. This probably gives them better protection from predators. Day nests may be built in trees where orangutans find food. Night nests are never built in feeding trees.

Females always build new nests. Sometimes males or youngsters settle for sleeping in old nests. Young orangutans begin practicing building their own night nests at age 2. They still sleep in their mothers' nests for another year.

Orangutans need the rain forest. It is where they live and find the fruit they eat. Even in a rain forest, fruit is not always easy to find. Scientists have learned that when there is plenty of fruit, orangutans will stuff themselves. They build up the fat in their bodies. That is when they are most likely to mate and have babies. When lots of rich fruit is available, orangutans are also more likely to feed in the same trees as other orangutans.

When there is very little fruit, orangutans eat more leaves, twigs, and nuts. These foods do not have as many calories (KAL-or-eez) as fruits. Orangutans use up the fat and calories they eat rather than store them. They are more likely to be found alone when there is not enough food to share. Also, orangutans are less likely to mate and have babies when fruit is not plentiful.

When orangutans eat fruit, they help to spread seeds around the forest. This gives new fruit trees a chance to sprout and grow. Without the orangutans, there would be fewer trees. Without the trees, there would be fewer orangutans.

Orangutans
FUNFACT:

When heavy rains come, orangutans build a leafy ceiling over their heads to protect them. They use large leaves like an umbrella.

This young orangutan uses leaves as an umbrella during a rainfall.

The future of this young orangutan and of all orangutans depends on people.

The biggest problem facing orangutans is habitat destruction. Many people live in Borneo and Sumatra. Those people turn orangutan forests into cropland for farming and pastureland for their animals to graze. People cut down the forest to grow palm trees in huge plantations. In 1997 and 1998 terrible wildfires in Indonesia destroyed orangutan forests. This left many orangutans homeless, and many baby orangutans became orphans.

There is still a lot to be learned about orangutans. It is very hard to study them in the wild. Orangutans are secretive and so well camouflaged that it is hard to know where they are living in a forest.

The first scientist to study orangutans spent months searching for them, but only got to watch them for 6 hours in all that time. The work of scientists is very important to the survival of orangutans. The more that people can learn about orangutans, the easier it will be to find ways to save them. Knowledge will be the key to saving orangutans.

Orangutans
FUNFACT:

Many places where orangutans live are hard to get to because of steep hillsides, big rivers, and huge jungle trees.

My APES AND MONKEYS Adventures

The date of my adventure: _____

The people who came with me: _____

_____

Where I went: _____

What apes and monkeys I saw:

_____   _____

_____   _____

_____   _____

_____   _____

The date of my adventure: _____

The people who came with me: _____

_____

Where I went: _____

What apes and monkeys I saw:

_____   _____

_____   _____

_____   _____

_____   _____

My APES AND MONKEYS Adventures

The date of my adventure: _____

The people who came with me: _____

_____

Where I went: _____

What apes and monkeys I saw:

_____   _____

_____   _____

_____   _____

_____   _____

The date of my adventure: _____

The people who came with me: _____

_____

Where I went: _____

What apes and monkeys I saw:

_____   _____

_____   _____

_____   _____

_____   _____

CHIMPANZEES Index

GORILLAS Index

MONKEYS Index

ORANGUTANS Index

Internet Sites

You can find out more interesting information about Apes and Monkeys, and other animals, by visiting these Internet sites.

www.animaltime.net/primates/	Aye-Aye's Primate Primer
www.belizezoo.org	The Belize Zoo
www.congogorillaforest.com	Bronx Zoo
www.careforthewild.org/education.asp	Care for the Wild International
www.chimphaven.org/gigi.htm	Chimp Haven
www.kidsplanet.org/	Defenders of Wildlife
www.duke.edu/web/primate/original.html	Duke University Primate Center
www.enchantedlearning.com	Enchanted Learning.com
www.fonz.org	Friends of the National Zoo
www.janegoodall.org	Jane Goodall Institute
www.koko.org/kidsclub	Koko's Kids Club
www.lazoo.org/mahale.htm	Los Angeles Zoo
www.nationalgeographic.com/kids	National Geographic Explorer for Kids
www.nwf.org/internationalwildlife/chimps.html	National Wildlife Federation
http://faculty.washington.edu/chudler/front.html	Neuroscience for Kids
www.oaklandzoo.org	Oakland Zoo
www.orangutan.org	Orangutan Foundation International
www.pbs.org/wnet/nature	PBS Nature Series
www.primate.org	Primate Conservation, Inc.
www.rarespecies.org/pmarmo2.htm	Rare Species Conservatory Foundation
www.santabarbarazoo.org	Santa Barbara Zoological Gardens
www.scz.org/animals	Sedgwick County Zoo
www.sierrasafarizoo.com/animals.htm	Sierra Safari Zoo
ww2.zoo.nsw.gov.au/zoo.net/gorilla/index.aspx	Taronga Zoo
www.kidsgowild.com	Wildlife Conservation Society